HAL•LEONARD

EASY INSTRUMENTAL PLAY-ALONG

Audio Access Included

Visit www.halleonard.com/mylibrary

Enter Code

4905-8917-8871-4416

CLASSICAL THEMES
FOR

CONTENTS

Audio Arrangements by Peter Deneff
Tracking, mixing, and mastering by BeatHouse Music

ISBN 978-1-4803-6052-5

HAL•LEONARD®
CORPORATION

7777 W. BLUEMOUND RD. P.O. BOX 13819 MILWAUKEE, WI 53213

In Australia Contact:
Hal Leonard Australia Pty. Ltd.
4 Lentara Court
Cheltenham, Victoria, 3192 Australia
Email: ausadmin@halleonard.com.au

Visit Hal Leonard Online at
www.halleonard.com

FINLANDIA

By JEAN SIBELIUS

Slowly, with feeling

MORNING
from PEER GYNT

By EDVARD GRIEG

Slowly and gently

SYMPHONY NO. 1
Fourth Movement Excerpt

By JOHANNES BRAHMS

CARNIVAL OF VENICE

By JULIUS BENEDICT

SPRING
from THE FOUR SEASONS

By ANTONIO VIVALDI

CAN CAN
from ORPHEUS IN THE UNDERWORLD

By JACQUES OFFENBACH

MUSETTE
from THE ANNA MAGDALENA NOTEBOOK

By JOHANN SEBASTIAN BACH

TRUMPET VOLUNTARY
(Prince of Denmark's March)

By JEREMIAH CLARKE

Majestically

8

LARGO
from SYMPHONY NO. 9 ("New World")

By ANTONIN DVOŘÁK

ODE TO JOY
from SYMPHONY NO. 9

By LUDWIG VAN BEETHOVEN